COCAINE & UNDERPANTS

Alan Bowne

BROADWAY PLAY PUBLISHING INC
New York
www.broadwayplaypublishing.com
info@broadwayplaypublishing.com

Cover photo of the author, Stuyvesant Square, New York, 1976

First edition: December 2017
I S B N: 978-0-88145-746-9

Book design: Marie Donovan
Page make-up: Adobe InDesign
Typeface: Palatino

CHARACTERS & SETTING

WELCOME FRALEY, *Irish dirty blond, in his mid-20s, a good body gone slightly to seed*

NICKY SANTINO, *Italian raven-haired, coarsely pretty, a bit overblown, in her mid-20s*

RITZ, *a black man in his late 30s, powerfully built*

Throughout, WELCOME *is in jockey shorts,* NICKY *in scanty black slip and jet-black panties, and* RITZ *in a disreputable overcoat.*

A Ninth Avenue studio apartment, midtown Manhattan tenement.

A room. Mattress on the floor, covered with dirty sheets and pillows. At foot of bed, a Woolworths' mirror propped against a crate. A shabby armchair. Clothes strewn about, of both genders. Entrance off left, bathroom off right. The sort of room where you only go to sleep.

Time: The present

PROP LIST

Strewn clothes: WELCOME's *jeans, shirts, boots*

NICKY's *skimpy dresses, lingerie, shoes*

A nearly empty jar of instant coffee, with spoon

A compact and hairbrush for NICKY

"Cigar box"(under mattress) holding a large (10cc) hypo syringe, point, plunger, and a ball of tinfoil containing a sizeable stash of, supposedly, cocaine (milk sugar will do)

RITZ's *gun (a .45)*

One black net stocking for NICKY

(Late afternoon. WELCOME FRALEY, *in jockey shorts, and* NICKY SANTINO, *in slip and panties, are crashed among the dirty sheets of the mattress, a tangle of limbs.)*

(A loud knocking at entrance, left)

*(*WELCOME *stirs, looks off left, blearily calls out:)*

WELCOME: Yeah? *(Silence. He jostles sleeping* NICKY*.)* Nicky? Somebody knock? *(He sits up; calls off.)* So what do you want? *(Silence)* You some Spañol out there? *(Turns over, head into pillow)* P R ducks. *(Muffled)* They should gentrificate. This building. *(Pounds pillow, tries to get back to sleep, can't)* Nicky? *(Beat)* Hey I said Nicky. *(Beat)* Nicky from Bensonhurst, from Brooklyn.

NICKY: *(Turning away, sleepily)* From fuck you.

WELCOME: *(Sitting upright; to her:)* Wake up. *(Beat)* I said wake your ass up. Want coffee. And a Danish.

NICKY: *(Burrowing deeper into sheets)* A Danish you gotta have six-and-a-half brain cells. Who's at the door?

WELCOME: We got no Danish?

NICKY: Who's at the door, Welcome?

WELCOME: Nobody. Some P R. You ditn't shop?

NICKY: What am I, a delivery girl? I had time for Smilers? I had Bernadette, was who I had. You had. The pool table. You had time for Smilers.

(Beat)

WELCOME: Shouldn't'a.

NICKY: Who?

WELCOME: Shouldn't'a sold that shit to her. I don't like where you got it.

(NICKY *ignores this, burrowing deeper.*)

Bernadette is very-well-connected.

NICKY: *(Muffled)* She's a pig.

WELCOME: Oh. But what we got *here*. Is this French. You tell people, you this French. Nicky Santino from Bensonhurst and you this cross-ant. *(New York pronunciation of croissant)*

NICKY: It's good for business so cram it.

WELCOME: *(Mimics her)* Craaaam it. Shithead Brooklyn. In Manhattan we say, cram it. Like that. Cram it. That's all. You it's craaaam it. This is what, a French thing?

NICKY: What time is it?

WELCOME: Four o'clock in the afternoon, I bet. Time for my coffee. And a Danish.

(WELCOME *buries head in pillow.* NICKY *tries to get back to sleep. Tosses. Sits up, stares at him. Examines mark on breast)*

NICKY: Bernadette? Is getting very weird. Every time I see her? She's talking suicide. So fucking how long. Can you talk about it?

(A loud knocking)

(NICKY *stares. Then picks up hairbrush from floor next to mattress. To* WELCOME:)

NICKY: See who it is. *(Beat. Warning:)* Welcome Fraley.

WELCOME: *(Jerking up, shouting off)* Fried banana! *(Pounds pillow)* P R morons. Don't know where they are. Or why.

NICKY: *(Brushing hair, indicating off)* Fifty times a day this happens.

WELCOME: In a future time? We gonna live. Like 800 Fifth.

NICKY: *(Giggling)* More like 500 Eighth.

WELCOME: No more nigger things. Here. All over. In my building.

NICKY: It's the United States of New York what do you want?

WELCOME: To be with white people. Of my own kind. Who speak English. Through their fuckin teeth.

NICKY: Splotch.

WELCOME: Who?

NICKY: You. Irish fuckin discoloration.

WELCOME: You love it.

(WELCOME grabs NICKY and they roll about the mattress, laughing.)

WELCOME: Hey. You got nice skin. For a Sicilian nigger.

NICKY: Splotch. And pimples.

WELCOME: Nicky? You make my teeth ache.

(NICKY and WELCOME kiss, lustily.)

(A loud knocking)

(Exasperated:)

WELCOME: Jesus and shit.

NICKY: I hate all this knocking. What should I wear?

WELCOME: *(Shouting, off)* Go away! In Spanish that's— *Ensalada!*

NICKY: The black thing or what?

WELCOME: This is what I mean. I would open the door. And there would be this spickette. Or this abortionface.

Or her pimp. Goin tengo tengo mirer. And you never figure out. What they're yakkin about at you *for*!

NICKY: Black is quiet, but deadly. You gonna wear the regular? Change your belt for tonight it don't show the hairline under your navel.

WELCOME: I think the Korean fag at '54 is about to tumble.

NICKY: Did I tell you? He likes it when you feel me up.

WELCOME: So who *you* got?

NICKY: Don't worry about it.

WELCOME: 800 Fifth is blocks and blocks from here, Nicky. Who?

NICKY: Bernadette's boyfriend. Only he thinks I'm a freebie. And French.

WELCOME: He tastes some of that dirt you sold Bernadette and he'll think you're Polish.

NICKY: Shut up. It pays the rent.

WELCOME: But why'd you sell her that filth? We got lotsa good coke here.

NICKY: Get off. We gotta get ready.

WELCOME: *(Rolling away, diving into pillow)* Plenny time.

(NICKY *picks up nearly empty instant coffee jar from floor near bed.)*

NICKY: Come on. Up. You want coffee?

WELCOME: Later.

NICKY: *Now.* Hope we got hot water today. I know we got no gas.

WELCOME: You ditn't pay the bill?

NICKY: No. Did you?

(NICKY *rises, in her skimpy slip, jet-black panties showing, and exits off right.*)

WELCOME: So where's the bucks offa Bernadette?

NICKY: *(Off)* I told you. Slipped it under the Super's door. Back rent.

WELCOME: I shoulda shacked with a Jew bitch. Wit' some degrees. In calculators. Instead of who, I get this Italian and Italians? It's well known. Are not money managers.

NICKY: *(Off)* Wanna be outa here by eight. We gotta make the rounds tonight.

WELCOME: Don't take *me* three hours to get dressed, Nicky.

(NICKY *re-enters, stirring jar of instant now filled with tap water.*)

NICKY: You're getting very standard, Welcome. *(Holds jar out to him)* Here. Your morning coffee.

WELCOME: *(Sitting up; taking jar)* So what do that mean? Standard is what?

(NICKY *rummages through piles of strewn clothes, pulling out one black net stocking and putting it on, as:*)

NICKY: Standard is: Hey. I wish that fuckin hustler would change his vest. Or his nipples. Or something.

WELCOME: *(Sipping from jar)* This is a vision disagreement here. You think. That a guy. Is like a bitch. Who pulls it in with her accoutrements? But no. A bitch shows her nipples every night and the customers think, I am so sick. Of these tits on her. But a guy it's—

NICKY: *(Struggling with stocking)* The same thing.

WELCOME: No. This is the difference.

NICKY: His titties are getting yellow. From the cigarette smoke. *(Gives up on stocking, rolled halfway up her leg, and picks out a lacy black dress)* I'll try the black. *(She stands on mattress, trying on dress before the shard of mirror at foot of bed.)*

WELCOME: I'm tellin you. What it is. On a guy? Is this: The more I see those nipples. The more I wonder about myself. That's the difference. It's a closet fag thing you wouldn't know.

NICKY: I know fags. Like the wrinkles. On your nuts. *(Into mirror)* This black. Makes me look. Intestinal. *(Rips off dress and throws it on floor)*

WELCOME: I'll handle the closetnose married guys from Syosset, you handle your own.

NICKY: *(Grabbing compact off floor and sitting on bed)* So? I'll do the face first.

WELCOME: See. The grottier I look. The better, see. A greasy leather vest and no shirt.

NICKY: *(Making up into compact)* We're a nice contrast, I always said so. I just want you should change. The grot.

WELCOME: To who?

NICKY: To I dunno. More something—Puerto Rican.

WELCOME: What, I should wear a Fuller paint hat?

NICKY: I mean like. Sweat pants, they fall nice into the crack. A half-shirt, know what I mean? A jersey cut off at the ribs. You are concentrating too much on your chest. We need more belly. And ass.

WELCOME: This is not the image, Nicky. You flash ass at these guys and they think you're pussy.

NICKY: No one would think this of you.

WELCOME: I am basing this on experience. The colder the act? Like, this guy is just gonna stand there? An object of fuckin worship and a total man? And there's more profit in this, is what this is.

NICKY: It won't hurt to tantalize. Like I do. That's all I'm sayin.

WELCOME: I know my market.

NICKY: *(Frowning into compact)* Maybe I should punk up the face.

WELCOME: You do, and I ain't gonna be seen wit' you.

NICKY: Fuckin we are—*seventies*, Welcome.

WELCOME: Pussy is *still* seventies! You gonna *pay*? To some girl? Who got a magenta Mohawk hairdo? And zippers all up her that get caught in the acne hairs she has raised on her greasy heiney like bean sprouts?

NICKY: On me, I could make it elegant. Poofed hair and a paleness in the face. The titties in a tight hard case. Like a shiny bathing suit top outa some 1950s. I could be a walking whiplash.

WELCOME: For snots. Who go to N Y U. And talk film in your face. Suckin *nouvelle wavé* And they shouldn't! Let 'em above 14th Street! Without a passport!

(Beat)

NICKY: Yeah.

WELCOME: Yeah what?

NICKY: You and me. We're yesterday. *(She throws away compact and burrows under sheets.)*

WELCOME: This is bullshit! We're early twenties.

NICKY: *(Muffled) Mid*-twenties.

WELCOME: I can still pass for nineteen and you! Can hustle til you're fifty.

NICKY: I don't *wanna* be hustlin when I'm fifty, Welcome.

WELCOME: 800 Fifth. I keep tellin you. *(Snuggles under sheet, embracing her from behind)* Trust me. Sticky buns. *(Begins kissing back of her neck)* Make love to me, Nicky. It's only good wit' you.

(Abruptly NICKY sits up.)

NICKY: I just wanna *move* right. Like with a grace.

WELCOME: A what?

NICKY: A grace. In my moves now, you look close and you can see worry. About the gas meter or the next trick. But what I want is— *(She moves her arm in a graceful arc, a single unbroken gesture.)* Like that. No fear. Nothin fake. In my moves.

(Beat)

WELCOME: Only wit' you. No other girl gets me off.

NICKY: *(Exasperated)* Jesus. *(She rolls away from him, pounding pillow.)*

WELCOME: *(Snuggling up behind her)* Only wit' you, Nicky. Why is that?

NICKY: What am I, a shrink?

WELCOME: Say you love my guts. And mean it.

NICKY: I always mean it.

WELCOME: Always?

NICKY: Member that time fuckin I cried?

WELCOME: Yeah. I thought I'd gone and hurt you. Got scared. Like maybe somebody had *torn* you or some shit and you ditn't know—

NICKY: Be quiet.

(NICKY pulls WELCOME on top of her, the sheet over them. They kiss.)

WELCOME: I would never tear you. Scratch you a little, maybe. Under your thighs. Lemme break away these panties. They're wild. Break-away panties.

NICKY: My trademark. Nobody gonna mess wit'me, right, Welcome? You would kill him.

WELCOME: Destroy his face. Smash his nose and wipe it with his three-piece suit.

(During following, NICKY *and* WELCOME *undulate beneath the sheet.)*

NICKY: You'd protect me? If I tricked a freak?

WELCOME: I can smell freak. I ever let one near you?

NICKY: No, never. You never did.

WELCOME: If some fuckin executive just bit you. But once. Here. In the soft under your tit? And left a mark. I would track him down, Nicky, I would.

NICKY: And what?

WELCOME: You look so small like this. When you arch up like that? Like some teenage. Teenage girl.

NICKY: What would you do to him? Welcome?

WELCOME: Curb bite.

NICKY: A what?

WELCOME: Jam his face. Right into the angle of the curb.

NICKY: The gutter?

WELCOME: Gotta, Nicky. Cause he hurt you.

NICKY: *(Savouring words)* Curb. Bite.

WELCOME: Yeah. Wedge open his lower jaw inna gutter. Forehead against the curb.

NICKY: Protect me, Welcome.

WELCOME: Smash my boot into the back of his head lissen to his jaw crack open!

NICKY: Don't let him hurt me!

(A loud knocking)

(NICKY and WELCOME stop undulating.)

(Exasperated:)

NICKY: Welcome?

WELCOME: Yeah?

NICKY: Go see. Who it Is.

WELCOME: What, wit' a hard-on?

NICKY: Jesus

WELCOME: Nicky, come on. Ignore it.

NICKY: It's drivin me crazy. And anyway we gotta get started here.

WELCOME: I never get. To have you no more.

(Repeat knocking)

NICKY: Get off!

(Groaning, WELCOME rolls away. Angrily NICKY messes with panties under sheet.)

NICKY: These fuckin! Break aways! *(Having adjusted the panties, she rises enraged and crosses off left, straightening her slip, as:)* Sucking Spanish I'm gonna yank open this door and hell your face! Fifty times a day we got this, now fuckin *what*! Do you— (Beat. A scream:) Jesus! (She reels back into room and sprawls onto bed.)*

(Enter RITZ, a black man in a shabby overcoat.)

(WELCOME jerks forward, then freezes at sight of object being thrust out in RITZ's overcoat pocket.)

(Beat)

RITZ: I. Hate. Niggers.

(NICKY *clamors behind* WELCOME.)

NICKY: The fuck is he?

WELCOME: *(Shielding her)* I dunno.

RITZ: I want you to tell me. Why the subways don't run right. Why. Must I stand for two hours on line waiting for tokens at the token booth? Can you tell me? *(Beat)* Because the city hired a nigger to sell us tokens. He sits in that booth and he goes: *(Gear-change into jive)* Lemme see that is twenny-five cents and two dimes uh that makes what? Uh, lemme see, I gotta carry the one and Jesus there's a nickel and *that! (Gear-shift)* Is the long and the short of what I'm talking about. May I sit down? *(Smiling, he sits in battered chair, facing the mattress, object thrusting from his overcoat pocket.)*

(Beat)

WELCOME: *(Eagerly; a gambit)* You want coffee?

RITZ: I refuse. As a category. To drink American coffee. got espresso? You ever notice that you never. Ever. See niggers in Italian espresso cafes? Why is that?

WELCOME: We ain't got espresso; But I know what you mean.

RITZ: It's because the majority of black Americans imitate. Like on television. The fucking most blandest aspects of tastelessism and shit that is orientated to the lowest common jack-off in the country. You ever watch *The Jeffersons*?

WELCOME: We don't got a T V. But my girlfriend's Italian. Expresso's in her family blood.

NICKY: What does he want, Welcome?

WELCOME: *(To her)* It's a thing he's playin, that's all. *(To* RITZ*)* I mean, you wanna play, right?

RITZ: It's educational. Not only *The Jeffersons*. There are fifty-five jigaboo sitcoms on T V today. You ever think about that?

WELCOME: O K, but still. We got cash only around here and not that much it would pay you. You know. To play this out. *(Gestures towards jeans)* Over here. In my pants. A few bucks but you can have it.

(WELCOME starts to move off mattress. RITZ thrusts object in pocket at him and he withdraws back onto it.)

RITZ: Like I say. Educational. Not in a good but a negative aspect. What you got on T V today. Is a buncha jokes. Written by sheenies. For niggers.

WELCOME: Rots your brain. T V, I mean.

RITZ: In a certain sense you could say that. But in another sense, it tells you what little nigger dwarf is currently a star of the Jews and you gotta be *stupid!* Not to keep up.

NICKY: *(To RITZ)* Get out.

WELCOME: Nicky.

NICKY: *Get outa here!*

WELCOME: *Will you lemme handle this?*

RITZ: *(Cutting in; cold)* Nicky Santino. Sometimes A K A Nicolette. And Welcome Fraley. A team.

(Beat)

NICKY: Yeah? And so?

RITZ: And you live here at this address on Ninth Avenue in midtown Manhattan. It's a coming neighborhood. The Hassidic landlord elements are pushing the Spanish into the Hudson River and planning to stick a shopping mall on 42nd Street. It's a vision of Hebrew paradise. Thousands of black whores.

Pushing shopping carts. And humming the musak. *(Loud:) Buying pop tarts for their pimps!*

(Beat)

WELCOME: We go to Smilers. On Seventh.

RITZ: I know that Smilers. There's a checker there. A big reasy Jamaican dyke. You ever notice? That in the hierarchy of black America? The West Indians think their shit is somehow of a finer texture that that of your average nigger?

WELCOME: No. See, I'm Irish.

RITZ: Then you know what I mean.

NICKY: *(To RITZ)* You hate your own fuckin color?

WELCOME: Nicky!

NICKY: So go scrape your *skin* off! On some. *Sidewalk!*

WELCOME: Shut the fuck, Nicky!

RITZ: *(To WELCOME)* She's right.

WELCOME: *(To RITZ)* She is?

NICKY: *(To WELCOME)* Give him. A curb bite!

RITZ: *(To WELCOME)* She certainly is.

WELCOME: O K.

RITZ: She's the brains of this outfit.

NICKY: Get *rid* of him, Welcome!

WELCOME: *(To NICKY)* O K, brains, how I should do that?

RITZ: Every nigger hates themselves. It's a fact. They hate their hair. And their lips. And their large erotic behinds. But as Eli Siegel tells us, this is not hopeless. May I smoke?

(RITZ lights up one-handed during following.)

NICKY: *(To* WELCOME*)* What do we got, we got what? Thirty bucks between us?

WELCOME: Maybe. More like twenny.

NICKY: Whatever, it ain't enough for this clown.

WELCOME: Fuckin why' you open the door?

NICKY: Fuckin whyn't you rush'him?

WELCOME: Fuckin he maybe got a piece!

NICKY: Fuckin he's bullshit!

WELCOME: Fuckin so *you* rush him!

RITZ: Look at yourselves. In the mirror.

(Beat)

WELCOME: Pardon us?

RITZ: Look. *(To* WELCOME*)* You first.

WELCOME: Me who?

RITZ: *(Acidly)* Stand up and look. In the mirror.

(WELCOME *and* NICKY *exchange glances.* WELCOME, *in underwear, stands up on mattress before mirror foot of bed. Pats his stomach)*

WELCOME: O K. There it is. Me. Just like always. *(Beat; to* RITZ, *speculatively)* You a fag?

RITZ: Each and every faggot hates themselves also. Just like niggers do.

WELCOME: Because I mean. If you are. Maybe we could. Deal. I mean. We ain't got no money. But. If you like what you see. We could trade out. Whatever it is here. That you want here.

RITZ: *(Gear-shift into jive)* You ain't lookin, bro. Inna mirror. Like I ast.

WELCOME: *(Looks into mirror)* Sorry.

RITZ: Now What y'all see?

WELCOME: A Guy.

RITZ: Good-lookin? Star stud? Fast food? Master man? Cock up? Fourteen inches and radar? Lookin *good*?

(Beat)

WELCOME: Sure.

RITZ: Well, he seem a little chipped about the edges to *me*, bro.

WELCOME: The mornings are not good for me.

RITZ: Do he look like he hates the fuck outer his own ass?

NICKY: *(To* RITZ*)* You know before. You sounded like you just spent two weeks at City College. Now. You sound like what you are. *(To* WELCOME*)* He is unpeeling himself. Layer by layer.

WELCOME: *(To* RITZ*)* She's upset.

RITZ: *(Contemplating her; nodding)* She's the brains here.

WELCOME: She's upset. Now me. You couldn't do better. For the money you would have to pay? And for you it's free? I guarantee—

NICKY: *(To* WELCOME, *staring at* RITZ*)* Forget it. This one's no fag.

RITZ: Substance. In her brain pan. *(To* WELCOME*)* Keep lookin. Hard. Deep. At yourself. *(Beat)* Now what is it you do. When you hate your inside right down to your feet? Do you kill yourself? Sometimes, yes. But mostly. Not. What you do. Normally. Is punish other people. What we got here. Is. *(Tastes the words)* Aesthetic. Realism. In action.

NICKY: *What?*

WELCOME: *(Trying to pronounce)* S-S—?

RITZ: Aes. Thetic...

WELCOME: Ascetic.

RITZ: Realism. In action.

WELCOME: *(Nodding)* Got it.

RITZ: *(Nodding)* Like when niggers dick niggers.

NICKY: *(Throwing up her hands)* Fuckin he got a religion!

WELCOME: *(To RITZ)* This a new thing?

RITZ: Like when fags dump on fags.

NICKY: This could be like. Tantric. Communism!

RITZ: Like when hookers sell out hookers.

WELCOME: *(To RITZ)* Hey look. I been with a commie once.

NICKY: I don't! Believe it!

RITZ: Or like when dopers deal dope to dopers. *(Hard) Killer.* Dope.

(NICKY and WELCOME freeze.)

(Beat)

WELCOME: *(Slowly looking at NICKY)* Christ.

NICKY: *(Staring at RITZ; to WELCOME)* Shut up.

(Beat)

RITZ: Like Eli Siegel says. Now he is the founder of Aesthetic Realism. In his bestselling book on this subject, he says it all comes out of this what he calls your self-hate center. It's in the plexus. Right about here. *(Beat; fixes NICKY with gaze)* Stand up. Find it. In the mirror.

(Beat; NICKY and WELCOME both stare at RITZ as:)

WELCOME: Do it, Nicky.

NICKY: What's he yakkin at us?

WELCOME: Just get up and look. Inna mirror.

NICKY: Don't let him hurt me?

WELCOME: He ain't gonna hurt. *(To RITZ)* Hey?

RITZ: I'm waiting.

WELCOME: Hey! Must be a hole in my skull. Now money? We ain't got. But you mention bad dope? Well, we got a stash here. That will show you the kinna stuff *we* sell.

NICKY: Sure. It's pure. Natural.

WELCOME: Organic. We don't touch or sell nothin cranky. No way. *(Points down at mattress)* Right under this. Can I show you?

RITZ: I don't believe. I have ever waited. This many seconds. For a polite request of mine. To be executed upon.

WELCOME: Stand up, Nicky. Look inna mirror.

(WELCOME sinks, NICKY rises. She stands on mattress, before mirror.)

(RITZ contemplates her.)

RITZ: Pretty girl.

WELCOME: Nice skin, hey?

RITZ: Luscious.

WELCOME: Hot. You want her?

NICKY: *(Hissing)* Welcome!

RITZ: *(Carressing overcoat)* I could rub up against her with this here scratchy cloth. Watch her jump. Be like steel wool on skin like that.

WELCOME: Sure. Go ahead. Rub up against her!

NICKY: Fuckin I won't! Not wit' a—

(Beat)

RITZ: A nigger?

WELCOME: She ditn't mean that.

RITZ: She callin me a nigger?

WELCOME: No. She meant not wit' me here. *(Rising)* See, I could go out while—

(RITZ thrusts object in pocket at WELCOME.)

RITZ: Stay on that mattress. Where you belong.

WELCOME: *(Down)* O K. Sure.

RITZ: *(To NICKY)* And you. You luscious. You suckable. You cream-skin wop all prostituted in your black soul. Look in the mirror.

(NICKY looks.)

RITZ: What do you see?

NICKY: Don't let him hurt me, Welcome.

RITZ: Do you see a high-tone tart who hangs out in all the pits where niggers can't go but inside her she is just the dirtiest nigger on the Deuce?

NICKY: I don't feel good. I'm gonna throw up, Welcome.

WELCOME: *(To RITZ)* She's delicate. Can she sit down?

RITZ: *(To NICKY)* Or do you see. A sweet young woman who only likes to go out and party with her friends? A fine young innocent girl who might trust the wrong people? And put into her lovely white body some poison sold to her by'a rotten chunk of fagmeat and some hate-ridden negro cunt cased up in vanilla ice cream! Which. Do you. See?

(Beat)

WELCOME: Jesus.

NICKY: *(To WELCOME)* Cram it. What's he talkin about?

WELCOME: I dunno. What the fuck you talkin, mister?

RITZ: Mister Ritz. My name. Is Ritz.

WELCOME: Mister. Ritz.

RITZ: *(To* WELCOME*)* So show me.

WELCOME: Sure. *(Beat)* Who?

RITZ: This. Organic. Stash you got.

WELCOME: *(Reaching under mattress)* Sure!

NICKY: Can I sit down?

RITZ: *(To* NICKY*)* Roll up that slip.

(Slowly NICKY *does so, to just under her breasts.)*

WELCOME: *(Taking cigar box from under mattress)* Here
it is. *(Opens box, takes out fit and a ball of aluminum foil)*
This. Will knock your socks off. Only the best here.
With no impurities. *(Opening foil)* Coke this fine? It's
the circles we travel in, you know? You gotta have the
best.

NICKY: *(Nervously trying to pose; to* RITZ*)* This what you
want?

RITZ: *(Exploding; to* NICKY*) Look! In the mirror! (To*
WELCOME*: calm)* I see you have the implements. To
protect. Your fine, straight, un-niggered noses?

WELCOME: *(Spreading things out)* Right. A 10 C C hypo.
Syringe and plunger. Cause to shoot cocaine is cleaner.
And more economical. Up the nose you lose a lot, Coke
this fine should not be wasted. *(Pauses)* I need some
water.

RITZ: *(To* NICKY*)* Lookin so *fine*, baby. ooooh-*eeee!* *(Cold)*
That. Is nigger talk. *(To* WELCOME*)* Use that, what is
that? In the jar. Is that coffee?

WELCOME: Yeah, but—

RITZ: Use it.

WELCOME: But it's instant! I mean, water's better. You
don't want it pure?

RITZ: It ain't *for* me, nigger.

(Beat)

NICKY: *(Dropping slip)* Welcome? What does he mean?

RITZ: *(To NICKY) Tighten up!*

(NICKY hastily pulls up slip.)

RITZ: Find your self-hate center!

(NICKY stares wide-eyed into mirror.)

RITZ: *(To WELCOME)* Looks like a lot of coke. A dangerous amount of that. You two got the reputation. Of always you got lots of good coke. Bernadette thought so. *(Beat)* She usta mention you. To her daddy.

(Beat)

NICKY: *(Into mirror)* I mean, what does he mean?

WELCOME: Her Daddy?

RITZ: *(Chuckling, to WELCOME; indicating NICKY)* I *like* them undies.

WELCOME: It's. Her trademark. Those black underpants.

RITZ: *(Excited)* I don't *believe* it. Lookit the way that silk rounds out her ass. Lookit that.

WELCOME: *(Surreptitiously putting away dope)* Hot hey? They're break-aways. Whyn't you have her rip 'em off?

RITZ: Make her. *Nekkid?*

WELCOME: Yeah. Why not?

RITZ: Nekkid as a jaybird?

WELCOME: Bare-ass nude and stripped!

RITZ: *(Gear-shift; to WELCOME)* You ain't doin what I ast, bro.

WELCOME: *(Freezes)* Huh?

RITZ: *(To* NICKY*)* Keep lookin for it. Midway tween your titties and your tight black undies. Your self-hate center.

NICKY: My who?

RITZ: *(To* WELCOME*)* Take out that syringe. And the spoon. If it's as pure as you say, it will not need cooking.

WELCOME: Look, Mr Ritz. I can't put no instant Folgers in this stuff. It offends me on this very professional level—

RITZ: Eli Siegel says that coffee too is a drug. Now Aesthetic Realists. Got no truck with the chemicals that perforate America.

WELCOME: What's it called again? S-S—?

RITZ: Aesthetic. Realism.

WELCOME: Yeah. You know, me and Nicky we might wanna join this thing. You gonna have a meeting sometime soon?

RITZ: You gotta be a registered voter.

WELCOME: Huh?

RITZ: Aesthetic Realists *vote*, sucker! *(No pause; to* NICKY*)* You got a paperthin dress by Mary Quant?

NICKY: The fuck who?

RITZ: No, not you. You got you got you got these hook. rags! You would just *slut* yourself at one of our meetings! Cause all *you* got. Is some dirty black undies and a hate center that you! Can't find. *(To* WELCOME, *conspiratorial)* We'll talk when she finds it.

WELCOME: We will?

RITZ: I got a proposition for you.

WELCOME: Great! *(To* NICKY*)* Find it.

NICKY: Find *what*?

WELCOME: Your plexus!

NICKY: O K! *(Pointing)* Its right here. Between my breasts?

RITZ: It's a little lower than that, missy.

NICKY: *(Pointing lower)* Here?

RITZ: Lower. Don't you *feel* it?

NICKY: *(Pointing lower still)* Oh sure. Right here. It's right here. *(To* WELCOME*)* Where he said. All like in my plexus.

WELCOME: *(To* RITZ*)* They teach you this at these meetings? Fuckin that is the most amazing thing—

RITZ: *(To* WELCOME*)* Shut up. Dull that point.

WELCOME: Do what?

RITZ: Stick that needle in your mattress!

WELCOME: Are you nuts?

NICKY: Welcome! Do what he says.

WELCOME: This is fuckin the nutsiest—

NICKY: Do it, dickhead!

WELCOME: *(Springing to his feet)* Shut up! You got us into this!

NICKY: *(Jerking round to face him)* Mouth! What are you talkin? *Mouth!* All over your face!

(NICKY *and* WELCOME *are nose to nose.)*

WELCOME: This nutzo is *your* fault!

NICKY: Your guts! Are fag-O! To your *knees!*

RITZ: *(Cutting in; cold)* Poke your nails in his eggs.

(NICKY *and* WELCOME *freeze, looking at* RITZ.*)*

RITZ: Those are soft-boil eggs. In his sockets. *(Beat; to* WELCOME*)* Now that she has found her center, she can squat on that bed and we can proceed to negotiate.

WELCOME: *(To* NICKY*)* Squat.

NICKY: *(To* WELCOME, *looking at* RITZ*)* Fuck this.

WELCOME: Do what he says, Nicky.

RITZ: All right, missy. So stand there. And describe it to me.

NICKY: Describe—?

RITZ: Your hate center. Is like what? A two-sided mouth?

NICKY: *(Backing away on mattress; to* WELCOME*)* What's his problem? Sickle-head tissues? Some genital thing of negroes?

RITZ: One side opens out, the other side opens in. Razor-sharp teeth in those mouths. One mouth rips up the people around you, and the other mouth rips up your own insides. *(To* WELCOME*)* Put your hand on it.

NICKY: *(Halting)* He's twisted. A whole lot worse. Than I thought.

WELCOME: *(Putting his hand to her; to* RITZ*)* Here?

RITZ: Feel it? A row of baby sharp teeth under that suckable belly?

WELCOME: Yeah?

RITZ: *Watch your fingers now!*

WELCOME: *(Hastily withdrawing hand)* Jesus!

RITZ: You feel it?

WELCOME: Yeah.

NICKY: Fuck you, Welcome!

RITZ: *(Thrusting object in overcoat pocket)* She better squat.

(NICKY *squats.* WELCOME *descends to his knees*)

NICKY: He thinks a woman's vaginal area. Got teeth. Welcome? This is a Freud thing. He got. A bad problem.

WELCOME: *(To* RITZ*)* Yeah? Say, Mr Ritz. We can help you get over it.

RITZ: You can help. Me?

WELCOME: We're experts. Sincerely.

RITZ: But I have come. To help *you.*

(RITZ *abruptly stands;* NICKY *and* WELCOME *react.*)

RITZ: Eli Siegel suggests. In his chapter on marital relations? That you clear your head of fantasy and concentrate on your woman's needs. If you got homosex or rapism—me, it was rapism? If you got this on your mind, what you do is use your knee. Or your elbow. And totally please the woman and don't think about yourself. It's the same with your race. You must mentalize yourself away from it. You must denigrify, you must deyidify, you must despickify your own ass and reach the perfection of Americanism. So I have got my help. I don't need your help. *(He just as abruptly sits down again.)* I got a proposition for you two.

NICKY: *(Staring at* RITZ*)* This is a .dream. We're at Disneyland.

WELCOME: *(To* RITZ*)* I am always! Ready to do business. So hit me wit' this. Proposition here.

RITZ: I want that point to be dull, bro. So it hurts. Now jab that needle into your mattress and while you do that? I will explain the beauty of this thing.

WELCOME: *(Holding fit, at a loss)* Jesus.

NICKY: Don't do it.

WELCOME: You said before to do it!

NICKY: Don't do it, dumbshit!

RITZ: *(Thrusting object in pocket)* Somethin here? Is burnin a hole in my pocket.

WELCOME: O K! *(He rips back sheet, wondering where to plunge needle as:)*

RITZ: *(To both of them)* I give you an option. That is a sizey stash of cocaine. A concentrated dose of that could be fatal. But maybe not. *(Beat; to NICKY)* It's a chance, missy. A better chance than you gave. Bernadette.

(NICKY and WELCOME both freeze.)

NICKY: I don't know some Bernadette!

WELCOME: God, mister, you can't—

RITZ: *(To WELCOME)* *Skin pop your mattress! Dull that point!*

(WELCOME jabs point into mattress.)

RITZ: *(To NICKY)* You hear that? Did you hear it go in?

WELCOME: *(Withdrawing it and looking at it)* Jesus. I musta barbed it.

NICKY: *(In tears)* You got the wrong party, mister.

RITZ: Oh no. I don't.

WELCOME: *(Examining point)* Musta hit a spring or some shit.

NICKY: Please, mister—

RITZ: *(To WELCOME)* You ready to shoot up your woman? With a big jolt of cocaine?

NICKY: No!

RITZ: *(Again thrusting object in pocket)* You wanna die for sure? Missy?

(Beat)

WELCOME: We. Gotta do it, Nicky.

NICKY: *(Hands over her face)* Turn off the movie, Welcome.

WELCOME: You got a tolerance. It could be O K.

RITZ: Right. You never know. That' the *beauty* of it. *(Hard, to* WELCOME*)* I want you to scoop a heaping spoonful of that coke into that coffee jar, mix it up, and get as much of it as you can into that big dropper. *(To* NICKY*)* I want you to tie yourself off.

WELCOME: *(Holding up spoonful of dope)* This enough?

*(*RITZ *nods at* WELCOME. WELCOME *deposits coke in jar and mixes.)*

RITZ: *(To* WELCOME*)* Another.

WELCOME: It'll clog the point!

RITZ: You said it was pure, bro.

WELCOME: *(Doing another)* It *is* pure. This is no option!

RITZ: *(To* NICKY*)* I said tie yourself off, whorebitch.

NICKY: I won't

WELCOME: Look. Mr Ritz. It wadn't— If Bernadette is sick or somethin? Then it wadn't Nicky's fault. It was her source. She ditn't know. She just sorta passed it on.

RITZ: She got it off. A well-known nigger?

WELCOME: Actually I think he's Jewish.

RITZ: I knew there was a Kike behind it.

WELCOME: So it wadn't her fault. If I hadda been around, I wouldn't'a let her do it.

RITZ: *(To* NICKY*)* Peel off that stocking.

NICKY: *(Dropping her hands)* What for? You'll cack us anyway.

WELCOME: Fuckin that's right.

RITZ: No. If she makes it, I will just bid you adieu and walk on out of here. Bernadette's daddy has agreed that you may have this small chance you did not give his daughter.

(Beat)

WELCOME: Nicky? It's a chance.

RITZ: Bro, is it broken down?

WELCOME: *(Examining jar)* Yeah. Mostly.

RITZ: Good. Now peel that nylon off your whore. Tie her off with it.

(WELCOME places it in jar and reaches for NICKY.)

WELCOME: Come on, Nicky.

NICKY: *(Pushing him away)* No way! *(Grabbing pillow, she curls into a ball, face buried.)*

WELCOME: *(To RITZ)* What I should do?

RITZ: What I tell you to.

WELCOME: *(Pulling at NICKY)* Jesus. Nicky? Trust me.

NICKY: *(Still curled; muffled)* Get away from me.

WELCOME: *(Same)* It'll be O K.

NICKY: No

(NICKY kicks at WELCOME. They struggle. RITZ watches, unmoving.)

WELCOME: I told you not to sell her that shit!

NICKY: *(Sobbing)* Dont hurt me!

WELCOME: I told you the bitch was connected! *(He pulls off her stocking and falls back.)*

(NICKY scrambles across mattress; to RITZ:)

NICKY: She dead?

RITZ: So you got it off a well-known Kike.

NICKY: *Fuckin is she dead?*

(Beat)

RITZ: I believe it happened in the back of a cab. Girl vomited all over that cab. Then she went into convulsions. Cabbie didn't want no trouble and pulled her outa there. Left her in the gutter, convulsing all over that street. Bernadette died, Nicky. Trying to shinny up a no-parking sign.

(Beat)

NICKY: *(Low; to herself)* God Jesus.

RITZ: *(To* WELCOME*)* Now if I see a Jew. Like in the summer? Like on a subway? I go to another car. Those five layers of coats they wear? Those stupid hats? With the greasy hairlocks? They stink.

WELCOME: And they shit money.

RITZ: I never will eat Jew food.

WELCOME: Greaselocks and they shit money so you should go for *his* ass! Nicky's source. Name is Shelly some shit. Hangs out at Playland—

RITZ: Pastrami? Don't give me no pastrami on rye. Eli Siegel says they got nitrates in that shit. He usta be a Jew. He knows.

WELCOME: And this here? Also *this* is a Jew conspiracy!

NICKY: Mister? *(Beat)* I won't shit you, mister. She was a dip off, O K? But I never. Ever. Woulda with knowing about it? Have cacked her ass.

WELCOME: So why did you sell her that mess? You coulda traded this here.

NICKY: Cause—I dunno. Cause—I ditn't think about it.

WELCOME: Everywhere you look! And they shit money!

NICKY: She was just. So sucking *free*! All the time I see this bitch, she is goin from a limo into some building and usually? She hardly even touch the sidewalk. Just whisk in and whisk out and "How are you, Nicky?" Like that. With that voice. Like: "Testing? Testing? Will they play Talking Heads for me? Will you help me kill myself?" Always yakking suicide and then she'd lift up her hand and— *(Makes a graceful motion with arm)* — wave to somebody in the crowd. It was a T V show to her. I don't say she hated me. She ditn't hate nobody. What it was, I ditn't fuckin *exist* for the girl! You get me? You're black, you don't need a map on this.

RITZ: *(Looking around)* Who's black?

NICKY: Mister—

RITZ: I ain't black. I stopped bein black after my first A R meeting. Just like Eli Seigel himself. When he stopped bein a Jew. *(To* WELCOME*)* You see a nigger in here? Besides yourself?

WELCOME: No sir.

RITZ: *(To* NICKY*)* So there it is.

NICKY: Stop. For just a minute, mister. And think about it.

RITZ: *(To* WELCOME*)* Tie her off.

*(*WELCOME *nervously does so as:)*

NICKY: Listen, mister. People like her, they never gotta put out, know what I mean? Not like you and me and Welcome. They never do gotta. It's a law. American guinea princesses? I know, I'm Italian. Only *my* old man? Ran numbers for some old *coozine'*. And all my life I'm watchin these ugly fuckin Bloomingdales bitches that are connected and still are wearin the modified Farah Fawcett curls? Walk all over people. Cause it's in the Congressional Record. Princesses of whatever race? Do *not* haveta put out. We! Like you and me and Welcome? We gotta put out *for* them! It's an oppression thing!

WELCOME: That's right!

RITZ: "Oppression. Is All Up in Your Mind." Eli Siegel said that.

WELCOME: So what does he know, he's a Jew!

RITZ: Now, bro. You hop on that big dropper there. And suck up as much of that shit. Into it. As you can get.

NICKY: *(Grabbing* WELCOME, *sobbing)* Welcome! Lay it out for him!

WELCOME: They shit money, mister!

RITZ: *(Thrusting with object in pocket)* Get on it.

*(*WELCOME *scrambles for outfit in coffee jar.)*

NICKY: Welcome! No

WELCOME: Got to, Nicky! *(Filling dropper; to* RITZ*)* How much they payin you?

RITZ: Get on her arm now.

WELCOME: Bernadette's people, how much? In one week we could double it. Right, Nicky? We could turn triple-time.

NICKY: *(Flat; between sobs)* The Waldorf. The Omni. The Park Sheridan. The Hyatt Regency. The Best Western. The Plaza—

WELCOME: We both can turn out for you! You oughta diversify. Your line of business, you need to do that. Offin people, that's what? That's *occasional*! I'm talking steady profit here!

RITZ: They got *names* for you two at them clubs you hang out.

WELCOME: They got what?

RITZ: Sick. And Tired. That's what they call you two. *(Beat)* You whores. Is old.

(Beat)

NICKY: *(Hands over face)* It was a accident!

WELCOME: Look, Mr Ritz. For this girl here? I would hit that street. Even and bend *over* for this girl. You know what I'm sayin?

RITZ: Bet she got *big* veins.

NICKY: Stop! His mouth!

WELCOME: I'm tellin you, what I'm tellin you is I would pussy up for this girl! This is I love her this is no fuckin hate center and teeth here!

RITZ: Big fat Eyetalian veins. Rollers almost.

WELCOME: And if you make me cack her, I would just be this empty can inside here. Cause she's in here, like I went and wrapped myself around her. I can feel her sometimes, like her fingers are movin around inside my fingers like I sometimes can feel her belly all soft and jumpy inside my own!

RITZ: If she dies, you would be dead inside.

WELCOME: Right!

RITZ: I know. That's the *beauty* of it.

(RITZ takes gun out of overcoat pocket and points it at NICKY and WELCOME.)

NICKY: Welcome, make him stop!

(WELCOME embraces NICKY.)

WELCOME: Mister. I woulda done anything.

RITZ: You got your choice, niggers. Which it gonna be?

WELCOME: Nicky, we gotta.

NICKY: I'll die.

WELCOME: Maybe not, Nicky.

NICKY: All my pores gonna close up and no air. No air, Welcome!

WELCOME: I love you, Nicky, right down in my mud. Just think of I love you.

NICKY: Don't hurt me, Welcome.

(WELCOME *lays* NICKY *down. Fit in hand, he crouches over her extended arm.*)

WELCOME: It's gonna be Fifth Avenue, Nicky. I promise.

NICKY: Promise me, Welcome. Talk to me.

WELCOME: We gonna get outa this, Nicky. And all our moves gonna be—smooth. And easy.

NICKY: Fuckin so nobody can touch us?

WELCOME: Fuckin nobody. From now on? No more messin around. We gonna go for it.

NICKY: All the way?

WELCOME: To 800 Fifth.

(WELCOME *rests the point against* NICKY'*s vein. Hangs his head*)

(*Abruptly* RITZ *rises to his feet, holding gun aloft, barrel pointed at ceiling.*)

(*Intones:*)

RITZ: Gimme your asswipes and fuzzy faces. Gimme your greasy garbage offa every suckhole. From niggerland to japhead. And your filthy degenerates and your syphilis and your Greeks. Your Armenos and Filipenos and your cameldicks and beans. Your stupid. Retarded. Rice-mouth. Toilet-head. Gorillas. *Yearning!* (*Beat*) To be free.

(*Abruptly* RITZ *lowers his extended arm straight out before him, the barrel of the gun aimed directly at the back of* WELCOME'*s head*)

WELCOME: *(Starting to tap in needle)* Nicky? It's a chance.

RITZ: *Shoot,* motherfucker.

(Blackout)

END OF PLAY

www.ingramcontent.com/pod-product-compliance
Lightning Source LLC
Chambersburg PA
CBHW070037110426
42741CB00035B/2798